The White Spider in My Hand

Also by New Academia Publishing

THE ALTAR OF INNOCENCE: Poems, by Ann Bracken

THE MAN WHO GOT AWAY: Poems, by Grace Cavalieri

IN BLACK BEAR COUNTRY, by Maureen Waters

ALWAYS THE TRAINS: Poems, by Judy Neri

Read an excerpt at **www.newacademia.com**

The White Spider in My Hand

Poems by Sonja James

Washington, DC

Copyright © 2015 by Sonja James

New Academia Publishing 2015

All rights reserved. No part of this book may be reproduced or transmitted in any form or by any means, electronic or mechanical, including photocopying, recording, or by any information storage and retrieval system.

Printed in the United States of America

Library of Congress Control Number: 2015930112
ISBN 978-0-9906939-9-4 paperback (alk. paper)

 An imprint of New Academia Publishing

 New Academia Publishing
PO Box 27420, Washington, DC 20038-7420
info@newacademia.com - www.newacademia.com

for Grace Cavalieri
and
my mother

Contents

Acknowledgments   xi

Poems	1
The White Spider in My Hand	3
Man in the Well	4
Onslaught	5
Twin Shafts of Light	6
Monday at the Zoo	7
Ten Seconds with an Allosaurus	8
Where Dinosaurs Roam	9
Passive Voice	10
Splendor in the Air	11
Of Moonlight & Wild Cherries	12
The Schizophrenic in West Virginia	13
Postmodern Jester	14
Little Gossip	15
The Wound	16
Death and the Rope	17
Playground	18
Captured	19
Moving Target	20
Two Days	21
Three Thoughts	22
Postmodern Jonah	23
Artemis	24
Amazon	25

Never Ask a Cloud to Marry You	26
Description	27
The Purblind Witch	28
The Mugging	29
Transformation	30
Children of the Moon	31
Marbles	32
Lucky Me	33
At the National Gallery of Art	34
Clouds	35
Peas	36
Hummingbird	37
World at Night	38
Vocation	39
The Call to Freedom	40
Cradle & Buggy	41
Recession	42
The Old Ones	43
Beautiful	44
Common Rat	45
Squirrels	46
Pond	47
Summer's Play	48
Butterflies	49
Death of a Mouse	50
Meditation upon January	51
Wild Garlic	52
The Skull	53
A Tangible Word	54
Apple	55
The Voyage Out	56

Reaching	57
Halo	59
Ode to Toni Morrison	60
Trinity	61
Three Bells	62
The Sisters	63
School Daze	64
Effrontery	65
A Pure Gust of Wind	66
A Diagram of Easter	67
Sugar	68
Confessions of a Literary Hiker	69
Night Sky with Crickets	70
Photograph of the Awkward Shoe	71
Watching a Movie about Killer Baboons	72
Fishing with Aphrodite	73
The Pregnant Hour	74
To Theodore Roethke	75
The Portable Altamira	76
About the Author	77

Acknowledgments

Grateful acknowledgment is made to the editors of the following periodicals in which these poems first appeared:

ABZ: "Watching a Movie about Killer Baboons"
Anthology of Appalachian Writers, Volume II: "Man in the Well"
Antietam Review: "Children of the Moon"
The Awakenings Review: "Two Days," "Summer's Play," "Butterflies"
Beloit Poetry Journal: "Death of a Mouse," "The Skull"
The Chaffin Journal: "Common Rat"
Cold Mountain Review: "Amazon"
Court Green: "Onslaught"
Crab Creek Review: "Never Ask a Cloud to Marry You," "Description"
FIELD: "Captured," "Cradle & Buggy," "Recession"
5 A.M.: "Little Gossip," "Lucky Me"
Gargoyle: "Twin Shafts of Light"
Good News Paper: "Of Moonlight & Wild Cherries," "Death and the Rope," "Clouds," "Peas"
The G.W. Review: "The Schizophrenic in West Virginia"
The Iowa Review: "Monday at the Zoo"
The Journal Online (Ohio): "Fishing with Aphrodite"
Kestrel: "Ode to Toni Morrison," "Trinity"
Lips: "Beautiful," "The Sisters"
MARGIE: The American Journal of Poetry: "The Mugging"
Mobius: "Ten Seconds with an Allosaurus," "Splendor in the Air," "At the National Gallery of Art," "Meditation upon January," "The Voyage Out," "Reaching," "The Pregnant Hour"
Parnassus Literary Journal: "Marbles

Pembroke Magazine: "Three Thoughts," "Squirrels," "Pond," "Halo," "Photograph of the Awkward Shoe," "School Daze," "Effrontery," "A Pure Gust of Wind," "A Diagram of Easter"
Pivot: "Vocation," "The Call to Freedom"
Poem: "Where Dinosaurs Roam"
Poet Lore: "Passive Voice," "Three Bells," "The Portable Altamira," "Sugar"
Poetry Midwest: "The Purblind Witch," "A Tangible Word"
Poetry: Works on Walls: "To Theodore Roethke"
The Shepherdstown Chronicle: "Transformation," "Hummingbird," "World at Night," "Wild Garlic," "Apple"
The South Carolina Review: "The White Spider in My Hand," "Confessions of a Literary Hiker"
The Sow's Ear Poetry Review: "Night Sky with Crickets"
Timber Creek Review: "Postmodern Jonah"
Words of Wisdom: "The Wound," "The Old Ones"
WordWrights: "Playground"

"Little Gossip" was featured on *Verse Daily*.
"Never Ask a Cloud to Marry You" was nominated for a Pushcart Prize.
"The Schizophrenic in West Virginia," "Postmodern Jester," "Playground," "Moving Target," "Artemis," "Children of the Moon," "Marbles," "Hummingbird," "World at Night," "Vocation," and "The Call to Freedom" appeared in the chapbook, *Children of the Moon*, published by Argonne House Press.
"The Schizophrenic in West Virginia" and "Children of the Moon" are included in *Wild Sweet Notes II: More West Virginia Poetry* edited by Ace Boggess.

This book is gratefully dedicated to Grace Cavalieri and to my mother. I also would like to thank Henry and Faye Davenport, Jane Dufourny, Kalani Gilbert, Paul Grant, Pamela Macfie, Dale Richardson, and Doug Thacher for their love and encouragement over the years. I am grateful for the support of my family, especially my sons, Malek and Howard. To my parents I owe everything I create.

Poems

The White Spider in My Hand

I.

The white spider in my hand likes
to pretend he's a rogue on the make.
I've seen him wink at a hundred women,
but only one has responded to his advances.
His eyes are like sapphires, she says
with a voice almost hoarse with desire.
Together they'll satisfy the angel of death.
Together they'll court the bones of the dead.
Together they'll unmask the accidental shaman
before a galaxy made hot by the stars.

II.

The white spider in my hands knows
only the blue mountains of West Virginia.
He sleeps curled in my palm whenever
the cedar trees are covered with snow.
His snoring is like wind chimes, says the odd
woman seduced by his glittering eyes.
She's curious like a squirrel on a rail.
She's skilled with dream and fantasy.
She's ardent with the repeated request that
the spider abandon my hand for her web.

Man in the Well

The rough calculation
of moss & stone does
not equal forty days

& the nights are as
even as the teeth
of a saw.

If I drop twenty feet,
I'll be in the heart
of the well.

If I shout, no one
will hear me above the din
of the gathering crowd.

If I cling to the bucket,
someone will pull me
to the airy surface

where a gray-eyed child
sings to the women
who await the new plenty.

Onslaught

I say "cotton" & the door creaks.

Sparks fly. Hot wind lifts my hair.
I am neither gracious nor kind.

All the eligible bachelors.
All the pretty women.
No one wants to marry.

Today I only need to spin in place.

The willow speaks Portuguese to me.
I am hot like the interior of a beehive.
I dimple & blush.

Words abandon me
before I can explain my theory of love
& how Rumor gives birth
to a baby with fourteen names.

Some say there were fourteen stones
in Virginia Woolf's pockets when she drowned.

Twin Shafts of Light

--for Suzi Gablik

I never promised the absence of riddle:
that portion of seed for the dove
that I keep in a burlap sack
like the words of God.

And I never fumbled for a way to lament:
the path to riddle's end without ever
entering the museum where the young thief
loiters like a cold statue of bronze.

Life is so ordinary, full of custard and
peas, that I catch my breath at the sight
of the aged butcher behind thin glass. He
reminds me of my Sundays, pressed like old linen.

I imagine his mother once implored the bright sun
to shine with endless rapture upon a tiny, wooden
coyote—her talisman and symbol of love.
Like a goddess she appealed to the elements,

but being poor she had nothing to offer except
worship—the zestful idolatry of the dispossessed.
Now I offer her memory the hard feet of darkness:
commonplace, bare, and calloused from use.

Monday at the Zoo

Heart, show me brave things:
the miracle of the captive elephant,
the tiny hoof of the gazelle.

That fat gorilla in the cage
weighs all of 400 pounds
& knows neither luck nor love.

I witness his overt struggle
with the attention he shuns.
His staring is a mode of talk,

& the zoo's buzzing with new gossip
spreading like honey on bread.
The panda is not pregnant, and no,

the ancient tortoise has not yet died.
We're all welcome to solve the riddle
of why the tiger roars upon the rock.

Ten Seconds with an Allosaurus

At the Smithsonian Museum of Natural History,
something fierce beckons me to consider
the comely shape of the dry bones so
carefully arranged by the paleontologist,
bones which artfully command
the darting needle of my full attention.
Now I pierce dark millennia
with one soulful glance toward prehistory
as fleeting exaltation becomes presentiment:
the blunt yearning for human longevity.

Where Dinosaurs Roam

-for Ed Zahniser

From silence,
the slow jazz of dominion,
creeping
& the primary juxtaposition
of *is* & *is not*
now decomposing within the radiant blur
of accomplishment,
divine & void of complacency.
Colossal dinosaurs roam for millennia
before the frothing ocean spits
the historic myth upon the sand,
& the eternal abounds
as the robust foliage of the
tree of forbidden fruit.
A tree made alluring by bird cry
& the first temptation to taste
& be wise. Now exile's children
make a formal study of Darwin
as the continued act of survival
demonstrates that Yahweh
gave him the heart to explain
the fragile urgency to endure.

Passive Voice

How did you find that beetle in the grass?
It's small, and I don't know what to say
as you offer it to me on the palm of your
trembling, outstretched hand. I see it
glint metallic as a ray of sun bounces off
the tiny domed back. Lizard food, you say
to me, but I decline your thinly veiled offer.
You've always thought me a reptilian
being, close in spirit to iguana and
komodo dragon. Now I'm satisfied that you
want to take care of me forever, like a
devoted monkey eating the shuddering louse
that was imbedded in its cousin's hair.

Splendor in the Air

This calm creates a viability like breath
though no stone will be moved because of it.

For years, winter filled the street with snow,
and I lived the dim continuation of frost in spring.

"No moment is safe," you once said,
and I uttered a cry like a mute on fire.

Summer radiance, tangible, green,
knows as many bodies as there are trees.

Oh, come to me during any season.
I crave the force of your bittersweet wildness:

as sudden as the blink of an eye
closed against a flying object.

Of Moonlight & Wild Cherries

Next to the outlandish sun,
you're the greatest source of light.

You make the evening desert glow
as if it were always high noon.

You can't resist the temptation
to breathe jets of fire into the night.

Now moon's shimmer approaches
as you descend the rickety stairs

as softly as the murmuring cascade
of History gently bathing old ruins.

The Schizophrenic in West Virginia

To rest here, I mimic the cry of Galileo.
It moves, I shriek
and that's why I must be still.
Like Goya's *Maja*
I recline nude upon the sofa,
wondering at the change in my visage
when I decide to become fully clothed.
Double my heart,
and I'll make a red fist of Being,
existence blunt and total.
The church hides nothing.
Carnivores and penitents emerge with equal tenacity.
God knows my dream of the broken chair,
once a throne to Cleopatra.

Postmodern Jester

The shade of the obvious, the color of newsprint
subdues me to be silent like a weed in a stream.
No chimes tinkle in the transparency of dawn
though everyone waits for a sign from the heavens.

For I am an earthen vessel containing remnants of folly
instead of gracious words to fill the blank page.
Blunt memory ties me to the gift of fools,
the ability to mock where motley is worn,

& all day I seek & retrieve what humors
the idle scions who swear by public oaths of trust.
Let me be the one to explain the heartless game:
the principle goal is to suppress one fatal joke a day.

Little Gossip

Truth and fancy
make your upper lip curl
like the brim of a hat

facing the East wind
as other rumors arrive
with the playful ease

of a harlequin's somersault.
Now wind and sky breed
a pair of Siamese twins,

but you only appear
complacent. You predicted
their birth all along

as if you were an oracle
of great renown instead
of a fidgeting gossip

caught in the game
of second-guessing where to
send each caustic word.

The Wound

you who sang of what
must be while promising
that the last song
would never end
have torn the thick gauze
from my wound
that place of hurt
where wild orchids grow

& now the fragrant jury of flowers
arouses the sleeping god
whose manner is rough
with stone age courtesy
as he inhales the pungent aroma
oh the beautiful scent
of what pains me:
these blossoms of rare pleasure

Death and the Rope

What matters is Rachmaninoff
and the cry of the wolf.

Never mind the rain's deluge
upon a hot tin roof

or the popping of a cork
at an unnamed celebration.

That rope is sufficient
to hang a man twice,

and if his name is John Brown,
the act will be clean.

Show off the noose.
Let Death proclaim itself a rigid

sovereign crowned by the loud
piano of liberating beauty.

Playground

All those years in the schoolyard
with teachers' aides shooing the children

And himself lost in a psychiatric ward
A child that never was

He babbles about the dark

How he enters it when he sleeps
or closes his eyes

That's when he sees the playground
Little girls with hula hoops
Little boys with Pokemon trading cards
They chew gum and make a game of cursing
Whoever knows the most bad words wins
And he tries to win
Shouts "goddamn" to his widening circle of friends

Captured

Embracing the dream's verity,
I crave more words
that are true.

Elastic words. And words
without roots. Words so dry
even the desert rejects them.

Solemn instruments. Wizards
of investment. Describing fiddle
& bow. Also, what occupies

the middle of the road.
The mouse wears socks.
Yes. He does.

Moving Target

-for Dale Richardson

From glaciers inlaid with fossils,
from the mortgaged remains of the oculist,
from the searching monotony of flies,
I whip the song into the shape of distress.
I satisfy the dead.

What a pity I am no longer ravished,
spent like a dimension of sea-green frogs,
or worse, their cast off skins
but measure all progress with a nod toward summer
while polishing the smooth glass of old mirrors.

That's how you find out how entire I am:
saluting the kindly priest who consecrates the Host,
folding the colorless wing of my heart into transparency.
I praise the first glad hour of work:
the depth of my trembling, the glib ease before dawn.

Two Days

One day he put a worried cricket
in the palm of my hand then hissed
"Sing!" as fiercely as a furnace
at war with the cold.
Was he talking to me or the cricket?
The moment was sturdy like a nail,
and I cried out
as the agile cricket leapt to freedom.
My empty palm was as cold as ice.

Another day I picked a sorrowful monkey
from the tree that grew by the water.
I swore I'd make a gentleman of him
long before the day became night,
but he scurried away like a frightened poet
before the lessons could even begin.
I tried to imagine the life of a monkey
in the wild as I froze like a statue
beside the tree that grew by the water.

Three Thoughts

After sucking the dew
from the petal of the rose,
I slip quietly into character
& fake a love of the dawn.

That's when I watch the eyes of the lizard
who calmly struts the mossy log
of a fallen tree,
& the sight refreshes like the memory

of a golden carp in a pool,
how I fed it grainy pellets
from a tall jar that once belonged
to a wise gentleman from Virginia.

Postmodern Jonah

He erases his own name
as the blue whale
of the State
vomits him upon the shore.

Who he has been
is a secret
left in the rancid belly
of the beast.

Now he is nobody
as he covers his face
to pray to the god
who created the whale.

Artemis

Morning. Then evening.
How she poses in the starlight.
How she converts the silent night
into the distracted play of Luna moths.

Her name is Artemis:
she who indulges in the negligent river bath.
She who publicly embraces a virginal insouciance
to stymie the feckless philanderer.

How she craves the glitter of moondust.
How she hungers for the midnight hunt
where luckless stages will fall, one by one,
& wood nymphs praise her supernatural innocence.

How no man may look upon her naked beauty.
How her slim elegance remains hidden
from the mortal hunter's eye,
his lust to conquer the fortress of Olympian reserve.

Amazon

Oh
the bright advantage
of shoes that fit
like the days of the week

though I often boast
that I once ran barefoot
over a field of jagged stones
without flinching or looking down

as I told myself the lie:
why it doesn't hurt at all
and the women all said I was strong,
more stalwart than a man at war.

Never Ask a Cloud to Marry You

Shelter the dreamers.
—Jack Spicer

All day the salamander quivers beneath the mossy log
though because no one sees it or feels it,
you say I am making it up
& I say, "No, heaven is closer than that."
This morning I touched the salamander twice
& it quivered then
so why wouldn't it quiver
when I put it back where it belongs,
in hiding, beneath a mossy log?
I'm sure the salamander is quivering right now
& I'm not making it up though I am prone
to invent a thing or two, especially when it rains.
However, when the sun is shining,
it's a different story.
That's when I like to ask questions any idiot could answer.
Where is Plato?
What in the world happened to Jesus Christ?
A hundred years from now,
will anyone be reading Habermas?
How many characters are there in *Middlemarch*?
Did Emily Dickinson ever meet Walt Whitman?
You get the picture.
I know you do.
Just like I know it will make you happy
to discover that tonight I shall spare the life
of a beetle as it crosses the sidewalk in front of me
& if fireflies show off their fluorescent abdomens
at the same moment, so much the better.

Description

> *Poems witness our existence in ways
> nothing else can.*
> —Charles Simic

The tree exists in the mind of Poe
who can't describe it because he's dead.

Blood trust.
The hurt legacy of moonlight.

May I describe the tree
as if I were Poe?

No. I lack the passion.
I lack the fury.

I can't elbow my way into
the black pit of his soul.

Oh: the tree eludes me
though I imagine a jagged silhouette,

skeletal branches as rigid
as the thigh bone of a primitive.

A tree which is no home for the fugitive
owl speckled with rat blood.

A tree which remains invisible
though the night contains

heart fluid
and the history of my telling.

The Purblind Witch

So long the night
of thunder and flash
and stridency among the trees.

So awestruck by the charm
in my pocket
that I dare not chant.

The river rushing.

The forest:
imperial,
urgent,
forgetful.

So much so that what passes
for song is torpor
and the reluctance
to summon the ball of fire.

The Mugging

Sustained: a chipped front tooth
due to the blow to her chin.

(She always reminded the children
to fasten their seatbelts, and
most of the time they did.)

Instant pain: a fist-sized welt, angry red—
bulging like a golf ball from her forearm.

(Evenings, she would boil water for
a pot of Earl Grey tea, serving
first her husband, then herself.)

What hurt: the tallest assailant knocking
her to the sidewalk, then kicking her stomach.

At this point she remembered how she once
read Robert Frost's "Directive" and wept
out loud over the passage of time.

Savage recovery: getting up like a stunned
pugilist, wiping hot blood from her mouth.

A day later the ever mindful police found
her stripped wallet only three blocks
away from the scene of the crime.

Today in the mirror: a half-closed eye
swelling variations of black and blue.

What she lost: the trifle of pride, twelve
dollars in cash, and the right to stroll
the evening like a tall, tall man.

Transformation

Deliciously probable:
my reincarnation as a praying mantis.
Female, of course.
Slender, with chartreuse wings
tapering like uncut blades of grass.
Equipped with lethal forearms
that grasp and imprison
one's chosen victim.
In this case: a common moth.
Decidedly male.
And arrogant.
Yes, rife with attitude
as he negotiates the harrowing maze
of the unforgiving night.
Add to the picture
a tangled bed of wild mint
growing beside a gurgling stream
that glitters in the moonlight.
And oh,
a tiny frog squatting by a stone
too heavy for a man to lift.

Children of the Moon

He rose from bed with a little cough.
More like a sputter.
His nose hurt.
And he was hungry.
He opened a window and looked out.
The moon was half hidden by a cloud,
and he was pleased by the sight of it.
Then he saw the children
dancing in the moonlight.
There were five of them,
all the same size.
They wore tunics like the ancient Romans,
and they held hands as they danced.
He wanted to cry out to them:
"Not so fast. Wait for the dawn,"
but his voice stuck in his throat.
He had to be patient.
He wanted to be kind.
He had no desire to disturb their rhythm.
How often do five children
dance in the moonlight?

Marbles

A glass marble rolls
across the tiled floor:
a warning to all
who would step without looking.
Children play here—
a game with loose rules.
Somnolent eyes brighten,
capture the moment's fervor.
Jewelled spheres knocking together
then shooting apart.
The essential quickness
of little fingers
abstracted into tools.
Playing. Simply playing.
The thumb is key.

Lucky Me

Once I became a mother I liked it.
I feel quite lucky that when giving birth
I was in labor only three hours the first time
and, incredibly, under an hour the second time.
I quit having babies because I was afraid
that my good luck would run out.
Sometimes luck is like molasses,
slow and thick and sugary.
At other times, luck is like running water,
so fast you can barely see it passing.
Most of the time I feel lucky and
wish that I could sing to show
my gratitude to the powers that be.
I would like to sing to the sky
and to the prairies of the Midwest
I have never seen.
I would like to sing to the Mississippi River
that I also have never seen.
I am grateful to the moon.
I am grateful to the sun.
I am grateful to the satellites
that enable my cell phone
to beep when one of my children
is calling me. Please accept my thanks.
I who am neither thin nor rich
feel very thin and very rich.
I am a woman in love with life.
I am so happy today
that I would give birth for a third time
if I could.

At the National Gallery of Art

The guards come running.
My children are too close to
a painting by Jackson Pollock.
They aren't touching it,
simply stand with their backs to it
while posing for a photo
to be taken by their grandmother.
Before they move away in an absolute
fright, my mother snaps the picture.
Now the guards are satisfied
as the scene shifts
to dump all blame on me.
My mother wants to know why
I let the boys stand so close.
My sons question me with their eyes
as one of them complains,
"Mommy, you said the museum would
be fun, and now those men are
after us." I nod twice and
smooth the hair on two little heads.
"Pollock used to place his canvas
on the floor and would drip the paint
onto its surface," I say
as I gesture toward the next room
of inscrutable treasures.

Clouds

The wide sky pulses blue.
Seven clouds are sailing.
The children beg for a poem.
Let it be as beautiful
as a prism in the sun.

The wide sky pulses blue.
Three clouds are sailing.
The children make a song.
Let it be as enduring
as the fossil of a mastodon.

Oh, a cloud is sailing.
A white cloud whips by.
The children gather words like plums.
Let them be as sweet as the forbidden
cherries on the uppermost branch.

Peas

A boy asleep by the window.
His mother stirring peas for dinner.
The wind pecking at the door
will turn away, outwitted.

Now the house is warm.
Now the child snores softly.
It's a quarter to six.
The peas swim in melted butter.

Gently, gently, so tenderly
the woman wakes the boy.
Her apron brushes his hand
as he opens one eye and laughs.

Hummingbird

-for Malek

Hovering above the fragrant cluster of lilac,
that hummingbird is as light
as a halved strawberry.
Though her wings vibrate like shook tin,
she makes no sound when she moves
toward the next bunch of purple flowers.
She's so very delicate
she reminds you of a paper lantern
fluttering in the breeze,
and this thought puts you at ease
like the colors of the summer day
when you first learned to ride a bike.

World at Night

-for Howard

Nothing's amiss
as little things stir in the dark.
Plaintive silverfish climb the road of the wall.
A Luna moth walks the screen of the door
with one broken hinge,
and the raccoon darts among the drowsy chickens
who only want to sleep.
Eventually it will be dawn.

The child mostly dreams to the song of the cricket.
As long as the cricket sings, he dreams.
The stars have little to do
but hang there giving light.

The boy parts the waters with a stick of fire.
He is the sole proprietor of the trees.

Vocation

Dazzle of clear water displayed:
Why am I suddenly afraid?
It is only a passing mist—
More ephemeral than a tryst.

Yesterday is mere nothingness—
So today I must count and bless
Every drop of tragic spray
That urges my light soul to sway.

Tomorrow is a wind of light—
So today I must bear the fight
To paint mist for posterity
And record it as poetry.

The Call to Freedom

The struggle for freedom is so subtle—
Yet is a simple thing to comprehend:
One vain man exploits another until
Their brutal relations can never end.

I cry in poetry; I cry with ink—
I delve into the heart of the matter.
I beg for the cold-hearted man to think
And bid the old prejudice to shatter.

I drink of the heart and soul of Camus
And relinquish none of myself to Hate;
I shall create the necessary you,
Now and now, long before it is too late.

I name pure freedom the life essential
And seek comrades in the existential.

Cradle & Buggy

A lonely cloud, high above cradle & buggy, gliding.

My ears are hungry for the division of labor
& my eyes take over for a while.

Two more clouds, also above cradle & buggy, also gliding.

If only the myth contained a strategy for survival:

praise for the horse, praise for the driver of the buggy.
Praise for the baby, praise for the mother rocking the
cradle.

How to introduce the baby to the horse
without making a scene.

How to purchase a very fine buggy
when almost everything has been spent on a suitable
cradle.

Recession

The tendency to swerve
(avoiding)
       the deer & the crow.

(Now seeking)
rejuvenation in the collective labor
       of the hornet's nest.

Providing
(comfort and/or a guilt trip)
       to the snowy egret.

(All winter)
capturing snowflakes
       in a brass bucket.

[The snowflakes...have melted]

[The snowy egret...has sneezed]

[The hornets...have evacuated their nest]

[The deer & the crow...wait patiently]

I know things are difficult.
Things are really bad.
What to do about things?

The Old Ones

In a solitary flash
a few old women pray
exultant
and kneel down in unison
ancient doves of peace
voices rising like a catapult
in an age of war
their folded knuckles
bursting white gristle
their bent legs
shaking gentle thunder:
a summons to gestate
and remake the universe
with a shout of glee

Beautiful

I only said it once.
My mother seemed
so sad and beautiful
that I had to tell her so.
And when I did
loneliness pierced me
to the core
because she became
quite gay and animated
when I told her
that she was sad and beautiful.
Well, I have been wrong before,
and I guess
I should be grateful
that her sadness
was so transitory.
Beautiful, yes, she's beautiful,
happy or sad,
and perhaps I'll tell her this, too.

Common Rat

What's odd about that groan
from the basement is that

it's from my own throat.
I've been locked here for days

with my eyes shut tight
like the wooden door above me,

and in the cool musk
I fight with a bin of potatoes

for a space to lie down
or at least for my right to nibble

with my head at the angle of my choosing,
marking me not as interloper but as king.

Squirrels

The wet brown leaves sticking to the ground
bird cry in the early dawn loud shrieks
as the squirrels mingle on the uppermost branches
which rock with a miraculous poignancy,
drooping with the mass of small beasts
who escaped yesterday's hunter—
a child learning to hunt from an elder,
a man who never misses except to make a point.
Now gray squirrels frolic in freedom,
taste the morning air as if it were a nut of pain.
The grim lesson learned of comrades fallen;
the branches bear less weight today.

Pond

-for Fred Chappell

The quaint little pond houses a thousand stones
and a school of tadpoles with golden eyes.
Looking up, they see my face ringed by bluest of skies.
Behind me, the ground littered with pine cones

invites the scrutiny of passing doe and fawn
who have a better grasp than I of what to measure
when pausing for a moment of studied leisure
to enjoy the summer breeze blowing fresh and strong.

Oh, I'm as limited as the brief span of days
it takes for darting tadpole to sprout thick limbs,
develop lungs and lose its tail as it trims
away its old life to attain the fresh voice of praise

for pond and woods and nimble, leaping deer.
Christ, let me love the wild tumble of wind
that makes the water's surface shimmer without end
beneath the opulent, cloudless sky: my richest peer.

Summer's Play

She's dazzled by the sight:
a tiny ant carrying a flea-sized crumb
of bread toward the collective lair,

though soon the ant will be lost to her
as it travels through high grass and weeds
to reach the voluptuous field of dandelions

so pleasing to her hungry eye. Today
she feasts upon the natural world which
only yesterday seemed an endless source of

irritation: she had slapped a feeding mosquito
against her forearm but not before its
abdomen had swollen to an overripe gourd

filled with her warm blood. As she mashed
the insect against her arm, its body popped,
leaving a salty streak of red upon her flesh.

Her thought of the moment: concern for how
the rising bump on her arm would itch
like hell within the hour.

And today, she's still scratching, though she
was momentarily distracted by the effusive
industry of the toiling ant. What's safe is

distant like a cloud or bird's nest. As she
sprays her bare arms with insect repellent,
she chokes softly on the pungent fumes.

Butterflies

You seem to like butterflies
so let me remind you
that I once wanted to be
an entomologist
& I snared many beautiful specimens
with my butterfly net.

I never let them suffer.
As soon as I trapped a butterfly,
it was transferred
to a rather primitive killing jar.
Under the lid was cotton gauze
that I soaked with deadly ether

which brought about instantaneous death.
Gingerly I would pick up the lifeless butterfly
& pierce its thorax with a thin pin.
Then I would position the insect on the drying board
while careful not to finger the powdery wings.
Last, I stretched the wings across the drying board,

securing them with delicate entomologist's pins
so that the butterfly maintained an attitude of flight.
After a week of drying,
the creature was relegated to my collector's box.
Nearly ten years old,
I was proud of the variety of the species that I caught.

Death of a Mouse

Her song is cheap—
a mere sliver, a lie
based on the certainty of death.

And yet,
the mouse gloats in the pantry.

Come see for yourself
the wondrous suck and pull
of the distant ocean
which is her strength.

Insert a needle
into the blue nerve of the sky
and you'll discover
the fit body of her god.

Yes,
steal the cloud ripped by pleasure.

Unbearable—
the August heat,
the first taste of the farmer's poison.

Meditation upon January

The sheer possibility of West Virginia days:
winter toughness, the clean spoon of mercy,
stolid ardor like a tooth is a skull.
Still, as delicate as ancient parchment
displayed in a city-slick museum.

Pure exhilaration: sunlight's voyage
through my bedroom window, its entry
as welcome as a prison key
turning in an old-fashioned lock.
The sky becomes monstrous with gray clouds,

an invitation to all birds of prey, yet I
will not answer. Neither will I seek the penny
of salvation marooned in the empty chalice.
Call me to a distant room
where a flying hawk decorates the wall.

Wild Garlic

I don't want to sit
in the shade of the maple tree.
I'd rather fight the weeds so
relentlessly nourished by the sun.
Yes, fistful by verdant fistful, most
especially the wild garlic
whose whiskered bulbs leave
their shelter of earth as easily
as a threaded needle is pulled
through a square of cotton.
It's uncanny the way
they smell good enough to eat,
yet I lose my appetite at the
sight of a plump earthworm
retreating into a minute hole.
Though I haven't been fishing
for years, in my mind's eye
I suddenly see the metal can
full of squirming worms used for
bait, and I hear the laughter
of my father.
The river is wide,
but I'll never be lonely.

The Skull

Shimmers, no,
winks in sunlight
the varnished skull
of the fox.

Now, the fierce projectile
disclosing
my fabulous debt to
the ever flaming sun:

Dante's journey toward Beatrice,
or, better yet,
my own thin lips glowing—
two red-hot wires

burning to be cooled
in that sacred barrel
of glinting water
lugged from the Shenandoah.

A Tangible Word

Gut.
The beauty of sin
once it's forgiven.
Solace
like the feathers
of a nightingale.
Muddy paw of a dog,
preferably a shih tzu.
A month or two
at most.
Michelangelo
reaching for a brush.
Sylvia Plath
in her toxic kitchen.
The insolent eye,
open and without trust.
A hedge
about to be trimmed.

Apple

I spy
a red apple upon the oak table,
and I yearn to tear its smooth skin
with my strong, white teeth.
I'm not even hungry,
but I exist to make a difference
in the shape of something round.

The Voyage Out

My heart sails forth like a ghost ship from Portugal.
Being giddy enough to defy raw luck,
I pass through the rainbow's vivid glow
without stopping to chat with the resident doves.
Oh, I'm a burden to no one, especially not God,
as I sustain the boisterous journey westward
accompanied by bustling angels let loose like
fortunate dogs roaming a clean city park.
Shouting aborigines watch me swallow clouds whole
as I continue to fly as free as a spark from an anvil.

Reaching

At first you wince
when the dying star
falls at your feet.
The feeling is a regret
like that hunger you
experience upon breaking
a jar of unopened honey.
You never meant any harm;
it's just that you'd
been buried in the cave
for so long and yearned
for a little light.
You never imagined
that the arc of your arm
would reach so far
into the heavens
or disturb so many things.
Within the span of a minute
you'd rearranged the galaxy:
sun, moon, planets
and no one thought
to warn you not to touch
the tiniest of the stars
made ever so fragile
by an overcrowded system.
You touched the star,
only intending to move it
from the Milky Way
to a more spacious realm,
but instead it fell

from the sky
as quickly as ash
from a burning cigar
while consuming itself
like the pain
that unnerves you.

Halo

The angel's halo is as familiar as brass knuckles
on the fingers of an escaped convict, and I want one
the way a child wants a water gun on a hot July day.

Being new to heaven,
I haven't earned mine yet
and glide through the eternal morning
as bareheaded as an errant bluejay
riding the winds of petty conquest.

How long until I earn the right
to celestial adornment, the quiet trappings
of a godly existence? No one seems to know,

though children cut from earthly life
before their time was up
already sport the angelic rim
as if it were a sun visor won in a carnival game
along the boardwalk of a crowded beach.

Ode to Toni Morrison

The indolence of summer troubles & tickles
her right beneath the ribs.
She's sure one is missing.
Not for a moment does she believe
that Eve was created from Adam.
No, it's the other way around.
Not only that, creation is universal.
Every woman loses a rib
in the making of something:
a song, a baby, a helpmate.
She owns the waters that lick the shore.
She owns laughter.
She owns the languid summer.
The almost ecstatic thrill
of bearing witness to blossom & strut
holds forth a promise:
the intransigent katydid will winter in her hand.

Trinity

Imagine an almost naked Magritte
wearing nothing but black socks
as he stands beside a marble bust
of Harriet Tubman.
If you dare enter the scene,
first take off your clothes
& don black socks
then stand on the other side
of the bust so that the picture
contains a nude painter,
a queenly liberator,
& yourself.
Are you a museum aficionado
or just someone wishing
to express gratitude
to a woman of supreme courage?
It is said that she suffered
from narcolepsy.
Touch her smooth cheek.
Reach for the warm hand
of Magritte.
Sleep will taunt the three of you
as surely as water attracts
the ghost of the moon.

Three Bells

-for Robert Pinsky

1. Sincerity

Cry to the rain.
Watch it throw kisses upon the earth.

A vegetative state,
screen of the mind gone soft.

Rain, heart, stone:--
all fall through the air without sound.

2. Curiosity

The bee of existence
exhumes the spider of sleep.

Silence touching my ear
like the tongue of a cat.

Oh when will the musician
destroy his guitar?

3. Brevity

The book is open.
The book spews words larger

than the world of beasts.
Abbreviation: *birds at rest*.

Dip now, pretty sky.
Release a hammock of cloud.

The Sisters

-for Scarlett

Sisters: jointly constructing a cradle of words
to shelter every stray thought of winter light.

Sisters: saving buttons and ashes
and the odd coin from the realm.

Oh yes, the beauty of their bond
like the whisper of silk when satin would do
or the pride of dominion over rust and steel.

And in the end, isn't life as poignant
as the story of God letting Adam name the animals
and Adam forgetting a bird with white feathers,
tiny feet, and indigestion?

The bird cried out, but Adam had moved on.

School Daze

I see it so vividly
that I cry out with wonder:

a six-year-old Brooke Shields
is being taught to read
by an aged Eudora Welty
who taps out words
upon a miniature chalkboard
with a piece of yellow chalk.

Oh angels that minister
to the moon,
unleash the heat of that room
where the girl stands at attention
without being lashed or driven.

And lest I forget one detail
I'll record it now:
a ceiling fan
turning turning turning
like the first wheel ever
invented by primitives
as it spins out of control.

Effrontery

Effrontery is a golden egg
from a white chicken
or dove cry as soothing
as rum in the belly of a pirate.

Don't be a cad,
says the pesky urchin to Caesar.

That, too, is effrontery.

In a world where a little cheek
goes a long way,
consider the asp of Cleopatra
as it lifts its head
like a renegade nun
in a cloister of shadows
before sending the Queen of Egypt
to behold the gracious luster
of dark.

A Pure Gust of Wind

-for my sons

1.
little child
don't cry for summer honey

the bee is generous
the day is warm

bright school days shimmer before you,
offering Melville like a plum

2.
little child
don't chase the eagle in the sky

the bird is swift
your hands are small

& the wings of a dove are
but a fraction of what you need

3.
little child
don't crave the forgetfulness of silk

the worm is a toiling vigor
its cocoon is solid wealth

yet the fabric you weave is cotton,
democracy's denim restraint

A Diagram of Easter

Love pants
in the anxious wilderness
of the self.

Why now?
Why not beat the shadow
from the song?

Still, *He* rises as body,
& ascribes raw creation
to the pinwheel of the sun:

caustic grape of fire,
pulsing,
its pattern of audacity

not unlike
the shoulder of necessity
which is

         also transparent,

    not thick
    like the light
    of the moon.

Sugar

Tonight the ants will leave their colony
to taste my candy.

The mere thought of their approach
is like the promise of resurrection
without the prerequisite of death.

I sing as I prepare a speech
to welcome them to my larder.

This song,
more than silence yet less than a whisper,
celebrates the certainty of sugar over sorrow.

Confessions of a Literary Hiker

> *Someday we'll live in the sky.*
> -Mary Oliver, "Boundaries"

Before morning I shall defer to the mountain
where the black bear gave birth to twin cubs.
Only yesterday as I studied a sonnet by Shakespeare,
the idea came to me that mountains deserve
more respect than the artificial perfection of iambic pentameter
because mountains shelter living beauty
instead of being a mere grid of words.
The mountain is a haven not only for bear cubs
but also fawns and baby cougars and even newly hatched moths.
Not a day goes by that something exquisite isn't born there.
Even the first winter snow covering the trail is a birth of sorts,
making everything sparkle.
Of course, that doesn't mean that I don't love Shakespeare.
I adore Shakespeare.
I love Shakespeare and Robert Frost and Elizabeth Bishop
with an ardor only matched by the certainty of growing old.
I'm not looking forward to growing old,
but I hope to be cheerful and a burden to no one.
That's why, before it's too late, I need to capture
the essence of life in a grid of words
as stunning as the birth of a bear cub.

Night Sky with Crickets

From here, blood rushes—each moment
a penitential swallow swooping past a steeple.
Watching the clock, it's hard to fathom

the chilling brevity of each second.
It is the man in the moon who owns perpetuity.
Days and nights swim beneath his tongue.

The noise of crickets harbors his
constant surprise. Little is known of his virtue
or the way he counsels the damned,

but your life is a mirror where he sees
himself. Inside this image,
death recedes, disintegrates.

With his fearless dust,
the man in the moon stops the clock
so that you may press forward toward dawn.

He says you are good, especially
tonight when owls call above the river.
He greets every crocodile with a kiss.

Photograph of the Awkward Shoe

Apparent beginning:
the hissing *whoosh* of seaweed
as it coats the shore

Fresh mussels:
glutinous bodies retracting
like soft caramel
on the tongue of my grandmother
How I pry open
three iridescent shells
to observe the sticky meat
bunkered inside

Gull song:
rich expectoration
fleshing the air with ease

Sun overhead:
white like Hiroshima
learning to breathe
in the wake of the flash
& as lonely as
the solitary beach shoe
washed ashore
on a day of pleasure

Watching a Movie about Killer Baboons

-for Sienna

The dog sleeps
with her head on a pillow.

She twitches as she dreams.
My own dreams are curious.

Night is day.
Blood the color of a daffodil

rages through my arteries.
The sun floods the pasture

of my mind with a pure light.
I feel positively Socratic.

Dialogue begins with desire,
and I want to soar

like a falcon at dawn.

Fishing with Aphrodite

The coldly astonished fish vomits the hook
then swims away.
Now we drift—this way & that.
We do not sing.
We do not cast our lines again
because we dare not
tempt the god to rise from the waters
& give us a piece of his mind.
No. We are shy,
so very, very shy
that we sell our boat
& go in search of shiny metal trinkets
the size of a child's thumbnail.

The Pregnant Hour

We say: days become years,
and so it is.
Time furrows the skin of my hands.
I age as I write,
yet I hold nothing in contempt.
A fecund joy fills my womb
where my children once slept,
and I imagine a new pregnancy,
a begetting linked to the passage of time.
What if I could crawl into my own womb
only to emerge fresh and clean, baby-sweet?
Poetry is like that—
a winnowing of life from obscurity.
Vivid impressions gestate inside me,
and I am calm,
know that I shall give birth
to a living song
before the hour's closure.

To Theodore Roethke

Arrange the festive daffodils
as if you were gathering
the intransigence of idle talk
into one luminous fist of fire,
and sleep will come
like the bold scent of earth
at midnight when star babies
sparkle above the darkened greenhouse.
The shadows will approve your daring
as happiness tickles your feet
with the feather of compassion,
and so it goes that you'll sing
of hothouse beginnings: the seed,
the tender shoot springing forth
from white tentacles of spreading root.

The Portable Altamira

With a durable sigh
I return to the origin
of humankind
where you laugh

at all caution
as you paint
our image
on the wall of a cave.

Heart,
I'm next to a bison
& sighing like a bird
with a broken wing.

Let me frolic
while you trumpet
your genius
with a finger

dipped in ochre.
Preserve our kisses
with a handprint
next to my breast

then linger
by the fire
we discovered
only yesterday.

About the Author

Sonja James is the author of *Calling Old Ghosts to Supper* (Finishing Line Press, 2013), *Children of the Moon* (Argonne House Press, 2004), and *Baiting the Hook* (the Bunny & the Crocodile Press, 1999).

Her poems have appeared in *FIELD, the Gettysburg Review, 32 Poems, Court Green, Beloit Poetry Journal, Gargoyle, The Iowa Review, Verse Daily, The South Carolina Review,* and *Poet Lore,* among others. Among her honors are three Pushcart Prize nominations. In addition, she writes a weekly poetry book review column for *The Journal,* which is a West Virginia newspaper.

sonjajames@comcast.net

www.ingramcontent.com/pod-product-compliance
Lightning Source LLC
Chambersburg PA
CBHW031202160426
43193CB00008B/477